BASTIEN PIANO BASIC

D0128654

PERFORMANCE
PRIMER LEVEL

BY JANE SMISOR BASTIEN

Contents

*To reinforce the feeling of achievement, the teacher or student may put a √ when the page has been mastered.

ISBN 0-8497-5271-X

© **1985 Kjos West**, 4382 Jutland Drive, San Diego, California 92117. International copyright secured. All rights reserved. Printed in U.S.A.

Lazy Lion

La - zy li - on ly - ing there,

Please get up and comb your hair!

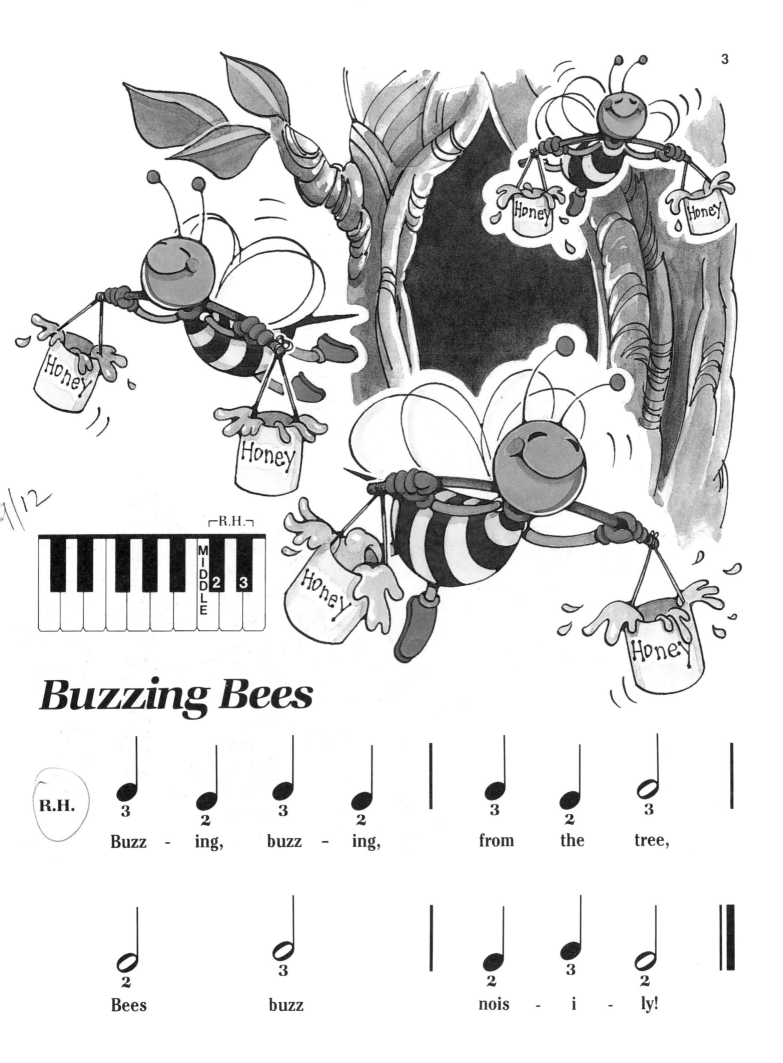

Buzzing Bees

Buzz - ing, buzz - ing, from the tree,

Bees buzz nois - i - ly!

3

4

At the Beach

Sun - shine spark - ling, not a cloud in sight!

L.H.

9/7
9/19

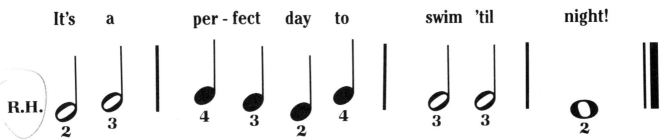

School Days

R.H.

1. School days,   school days,   back to school once   more.
2. Teach - er,   teach - er,   help us learn to -   day.

L.H.

Duet Part (Student part to be played one octave higher.)

C Position

Hummingbirds

R.H. 2/4

1. Hum - ming birds fly so fast.
2. Dart - ing here, dart - ing there.

Makes you won - der how they last!
Of - ten stop - ping in mid – air!

L.H.

Chocolate Cake

R.H. **3/4** C(1) D(2) E(3) | C(1) D(2) E(3) | D(2) E(3) F(4) | G(5). |

1. Please, Moth - er,   please, Moth - er,   hur - ry   and   bake
2. Please put   in   pud - ding   and   choc 'late chips,   too.

    My   ver - y   fa - vor - ite   choc - o - late   cake.
    Choc - o - late   cake is   so   spe - cial from   you!

L.H. G(1) F(2) E(3) | F(2) E(3) D(4) | F(2) E(3) D(4) | C(5). :||

Halloween Fun

R.H. 1

$\frac{4}{4}$

C E G E | F E D | E F E D | E F G |

Jack - o - lan - terns   glow - ing bright,   light the   way this   spe - cial night.

Ghosts and gob - lins   can   be seen. . . .   Boo! It's   Hal - low -   een!

C E G E | F E D | E F E D | C |

L.H. 5

9/28 10/17

R.H. 1

C E G E | F E D | E F E D | E F G |

What's your cos - tume? Mine's a bat. Look at Li - sa, she's a cat!

Here we come now down the street, shout - ing "Trick or treat!"

C E G E | F E D | E F E D | C |

L.H. 5

C Position

10/12

My Electric Car

Say note names out loud

Lively

1. Purr - ing   like   a   cat,   my   new   car's   real - ly   fine.
2. It's   the   ver - y   lat - est   mod - el   in   the   store.

f

I   am   just   so   hap - py   now   that   it   is   mine.
Sil - ver   grey   with   chrome hub caps and   lots,   lots   more!

Honk,   honk!

[*last time only*]

Teeter-Totter

Smoothly

Use with page 31 of Piano, Primer Level. **WP210**

Big Black Cat

Quietly

p Down-stairs came our big black cat, fluff-y tail and kind of fat.

Looked me o - ver with one eye, just as though to tell me, "Hi!"

f "Me - ow, me - ow, me - ow, me - ow, me - ow."

p Peeked a - gain with just one eye, then he quick - ly sneaked on by!

Jiffi

Moderately

f
1. Jif - fi's our poo - dle, he's cute as can be.
2. He sits and watch - es us all through the day,

He loves to play ball, it's eas - y to see.
Whin - ing and bark - ing for some - one who'll play!

Old Woman

Moderately

Old wom-an, old wom-an, do you want to mar-ry me?

Use with page 34-35 of Piano, Primer Level.

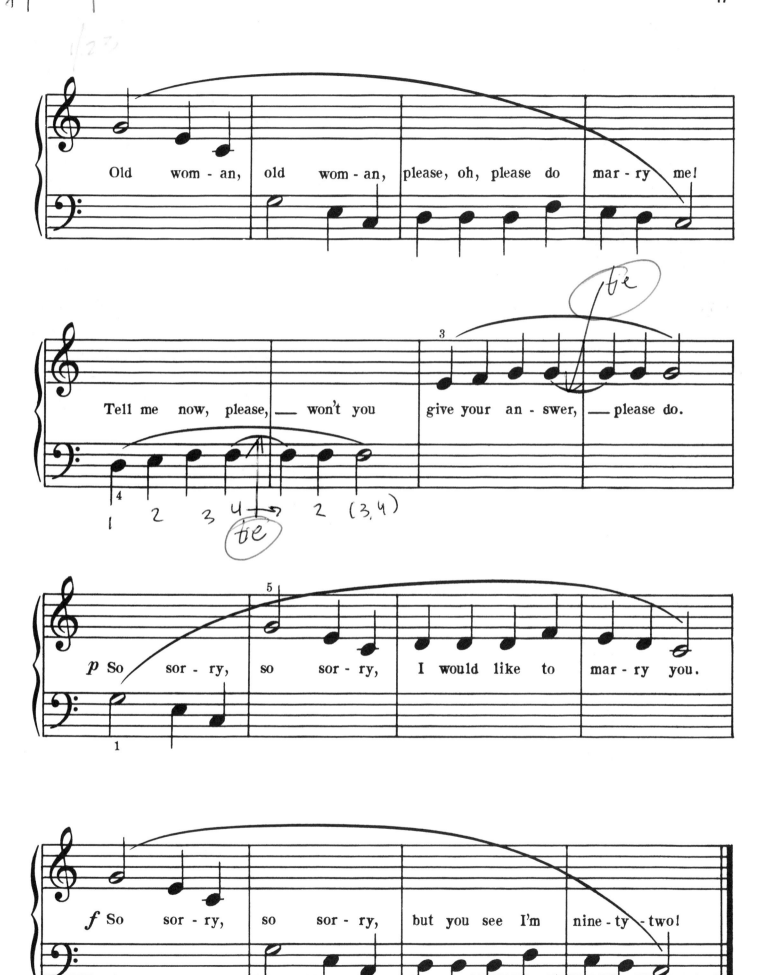

Popcorn Party

Lively

f Pop-corn par - ty, gath - er 'round, add the but - ter, one-fourth pound.

Par - ties are my fa-v'rite thing, lots of hap - pi - ness they bring.

Pop-corn par - ty, pop - corn par - ty, join the fun!

Seashell

Quietly

f 1. Sea - shell,   sea - shell,   sing   a   song   to   me,   oh   please.
p 2. Whis - per,   whis - per,   tell   me   things,   oh   please, sea - shell.

Sea - shell,   sea - shell,   sing   to   me   of   trop - ic   trees.
Whis - per,   sea - shell,   things you   know   so   ver - y   well.

Use with pages 38-39 of Piano, Primer Level.   **WP210**

Rock With Me

Abraham Lincoln

Moderately

p Once there was a qui-et boy who stud-ied all day long.

A - bra - ham be - came a man and made our coun-try strong.

f A - bra - ham, A - bra - ham, A - bra - ham Lin - coln!

Christmas Parade

Steady march tempo

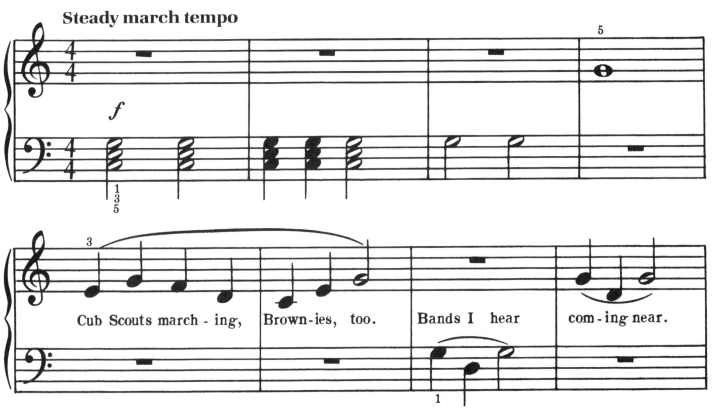

Cub Scouts march - ing, Brown-ies, too. Bands I hear com-ing near.

San - ta Claus will soon ap - pear. It's the Christ - mas P'rade!

Middle C Position

Yankee Doodle

Brightly

1. Yan-kee Doo-dle went to town, rid-ing on a po-ny.
2. As he rode in-to the town, ev-'ry one was star-ing.

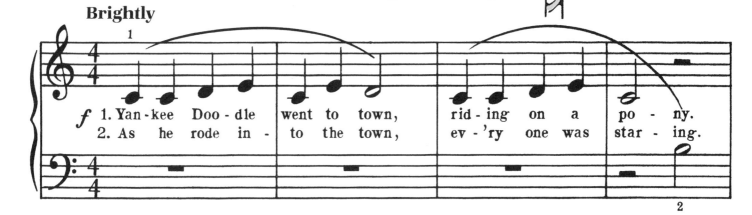

Stuck a feath-er in his hat and called it mac-a-ro-ni!
Dressed up in his bright-est clothes, he real-ly looked quite dar-ing!

Duet Part

Camptown Races

Lively

1. Camp-town la - dies sing this song. Doo - dah, doo - dah.
2. Went down there with my hat caved in. Doo - dah, doo - dah.

Camp-town race track's five miles long. Oh, doo - dah day!
Came back home with a pocket full of tin. Oh, doo - dah day!

Duet Part

stacc.

1/25

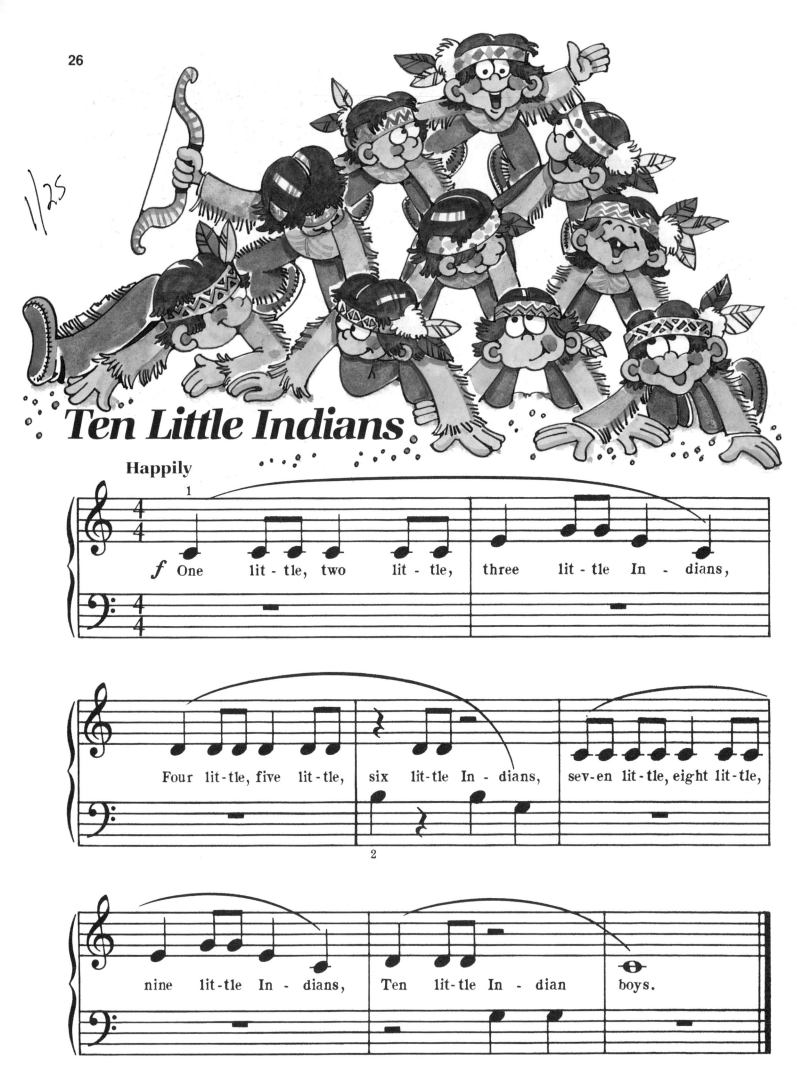

Ten Little Indians

Happily

f One lit-tle, two lit-tle, three lit-tle In - dians,

Four lit-tle, five lit-tle, six lit-tle In - dians, sev-en lit-tle, eight lit-tle,

nine lit-tle In - dians, Ten lit-tle In - dian boys.

My Red Drum

Position: R.H. 1 on D
L.H. 1 on C

28

People 'Round the World

WP 210 *Use with pages 52-53 of Piano, Primer Level.*

Lazy Mary

Arab Dance

Position: R.H. C
L.H. G

Lively

f

4/5/17